THE DREAMER

(A Fusion Poetry Novella)

Imali J. Abala

Nsemia

First Edition: January 2017
Published by Nsemia Inc. Publishers (www.nsemia. com)

Edited By: Verah Omwocha
Cover Concept & Illustration: Abel Murumba
Cover Design: Linda Kiboma
Layout: Bethsheba Nyabuto

Note for Librarians:
A cataloguing record for this book is available from Kenya National Library Services.

ISBN: 978-1-926906-51-5

Dedication

To My Mother Muhonja
Who inspired me to strive for a better
tomorrow

Acknowledgements

I cannot express enough thanks to Iddah Aoko Otieno whose words of encouragement were the elixir I needed to get this work published. Special thanks also go to Joanne Arnott for her critical and editorial suggestions, and finally, to my son Abala, who never tires whenever I need a listening ear.

Dreams

Hold fast to dreams

For if dreams die

Life is a broken-winged bird

That cannot fly.

Hold fast to dreams

For when dreams go

Life is a barren field

Frozen with snow.

Langston Hughes,

(1902-1967)

Table of Contents

The Dreamer

[I]

I dreamt small dreams,

But my dreams became big.

Father said:

> *Daughter, don't dream too much!*
> *You will contaminate your brain.*
> *Your brain is still too young;*
> *And for the love of peace,*
> *Stop building castles in the air.*

I dreamt big dreams,

But my dreams became bigger.

I said:

> *But why?*

Father said:

> *Daughter, you think too much.*
> *You are a woman.*
> *Women don't need to dream.*
> *Women don't need to think.*
> *Women do as they are told!*

I dreamt bigger dreams,

But my dreams became bigger and bigger.

I said:

> *Father, I want to study like Aiken because I can.*

Father said:

> *Aiken is a boy.*
> *A boy's brain has the propensity to absorb knowledge.*

>*Boys can dream and rule the world.*
>*Women don't, can't, and won't do that!*

I dreamt bigger and bigger dreams,

But my bigger dreams became gigantic.

I said:

>*Father, I want to rule the world.*

Father said:

>*You'll lose your place in society.*
>*Talk like that and you'll become a spinster for life.*
>*No man will want to marry you!*
>*You, a wasted-bag of confusion.*

I dreamt gigantic dreams,

But my dreams become colossal.

I said:

>*I want to have my freedom and independence.*

Father said:

>*Tiffia! Freedom? For a girl?*
>[He spat on the ground disgustedly]
>*That will make you grow horns.*
>*What man would dare to dehorn a girl?*

I dreamt big dreams,

But my dreams became gargantuan.

Father said:

>*What is this foolishness you dream about?*
>*You! You . . . .*

I said:

>*I want to be somebody, not a nobody!*
>*I want to study till my brain bursts with knowledge.*
>*I want to study about the wonders of the universe.*

I want to fly high into the depth of the sky.

I want to travel to faraway lands.

Father said:

Daughter, you've lost all your marbles.

Get your head out of the gutter!

And for the love of peace,

Be serious for once in your life!

I said:

I am serious Father!

I want to become a mechanic.

I want to become an engineer.

I want to build cars.

I want to become a pilot.

Father said:

Get your head out of my car and plane, will you?

Keep it in the kitchen where it belongs!

Keep it in the kitchen where you are useful.

I said:

Oh, no Father! I have even bigger dreams:

I want to become an astronaut someday.

I want to become a doctor someday.

I want to become a president someday.

Father said:

That will be the end of society as we know it.

The day women rule the world,

Will be the end of humanity.

Women work best on their backs,

Can't you understand that?

Is your mind clouded with dung?

I dreamt gargantuan dreams,

But my gargantuan dreams became even bigger:
That my dream will be my reality.

Father said:

> *Daughter, you are surely a dreamer!*
> *Know your place, will you?*
> *You belong to your husband.*
> *You belong to your kitchen,*
> *And nowhere else!*

I said:

> *No Father, I belong to the world.*
> *I am the world!*

I dreamt of my biggest dream ever,
And the kitchen was not my reality.
The kitchen was not my dream and will never be!
Father said:

> *You have gone mad child.*
> *Get your head examined!*
> *Go see Andigo, the seer!*

I dreamt big dreams,
But my dreams became bigger and bigger, making change inevitable.

As for my Father, he, too, was a dreamer locked in his past.

> For he didn't *understand* that change was inevitable.
> That culture, as he *knew* it, was gone.
> That family, as he *knew* it, was no more.
> That the kraal, as he *knew* it, was gone.
> That his mother-tongue, as he *knew* it, too, was gone.

Father yelled with disappointment:

You are truly out of your mind child.

I am out of here!

[He ran out to Mathare hospital, a nutty pen].

This reaction was simply because I dreamt a small dream,

But my dream became big and bigger, driving my Father mad,

Ushering his insanity and death.

For my dreaming, I, too, was condemned to an asylum,

My mental prison, where I am still dreaming:

Of big and bigger dreams, and will continue to my death day,

For if my dreams were deferred, it would be the death of me!

[II]

I pinched myself back to my reality,
But still dreamt bigger and better dreams.
I ran to my priest, at the chapel, thinking he would
understand.

The Priest said:

> *Good afternoon my child!*

I said:

> *Good afternoon Father!*
> [Father was as silent as a mute!]
> *Forgive me Father for I have committed a terrible
> sin.*

The Priest said:

> *What is your transgression my child?*

I said:

> *I dreamt a small dream, but my dream became
> bigger.*

The Priest said:

> *That is not a sin my child!*

I said:

> *Father, you don't understand!*
> *My dream became bigger and bigger.*

The Priest said:

> *I can't offer you penance for dreaming.*
> *You have committed no real sin!*

I protested:

> *But Father,*
> *I have sinned and fallen short of the Glory of God!*

The Priest said:

> *In your dreaming big dreams that became bigger,*
> *Did you worship other gods?*

I said:

   No!

The Priest said:

   Did you make for yourself a craven image . . .
   In the form of anything in heaven above?
   Or on the earth beneath, or in the waters below?
   Did you bow down to it or worship it?

To which I said:

   No! That was not part of my dream!
   *M*ine was simply a mortal dream.

The Priest said:

   Did you take God's name in vain?

To which I said:

   That, too, was not part of my dream.

The Priest said:

   You didn't forget to keep the Lord's Sabbath day
   holy?
   Did you murder someone?
   Did you commit adultery?
   Did you steal anything from anyone?
   Did you offer false testimony against your
   neighbour?
   Or did you covet your neighbour's house?

All to which I said:

   Crap, no!
   These things were not part of my small dream
   that became bigger.

The Priest said:

   I can't save your soul, <u>my</u> child.

I said:

   Father, you still don't understand!
   It is not my soul for which I need saving.
   I dreamt small dreams which became bigger,
   And bigger and then killed my Father.

The Priest said:

How did you kill your Father?

I said:

I dreamt big dreams,
But my dreams became bigger,
And taller, like Mt. Kilimanjaro.
These dreams made my Father mad.
These dreams drove Father to Mathare.
So you see Father, I killed my Father.

The Priest said:

Did you honour thy father?

I said:

No! I betrayed him. My betrayal caused his
death because
I dreamt of big dreams and my dreams became
big,
Bigger and higher like Nairobi's Times Towers,
Bigger and high like Burj Khalifa Skyscrapers!
My dreams were the floating kite soaring up,
Up and up into the depth of the sky . . .
No way down for such dreams, but up!

The Priest said:

Get out of here and burn in hell.
I can't save your sorry lot . . . you,
You, a dead soulless creature,
A wanderer on God's grandiose earth.
Your dreams are your death!

I dreamt big dreams,
But my dreams became bigger and bigger.
Now, I am condemned, yet again, only this time to
Hades.
But, I'll keep on dreaming and dreaming,
For a dream differed will be my death,
The death of humanity, an apocalyptic end!

[III]

I boarded a *Boda Boda* to my Member of Parliament's office.

Surely, he will understand my dream. He has gone to places,

And traversed the universe. He knows dreams, big dreams like mine.

He, the beneficiary of *Mau Mau*, of those who dared to dream big dreams,

Dreams of *our* freedom. So I stormed into his office with glee.

A picture frame of Kibaki's smiling face hung on the wall;

He, too, must have dreamt big dreams, just like me.

His secretary said:

Good morning Madam.

I turned around to look, but there was no one else, but me.

No one had ever called me Madam before.

I said:

Oh! Good morning.

The secretary said:

What can I do for you?

I said:

I dreamt big dreams,

But my dreams became bigger.

I came to see if his Excellence,

Mr. MP, can help me realize my dreams!

[Just then, in walked Mr. MP]

The secretary said:

This Madam says:

She dreamt big dreams,

But her dreams became bigger.

Only you can help her realize them.

Mr. MP said:

Madam!

Are you one of my subjects?

[I nodded]

Great! How can I be of service to you?

I said:

I dreamt big dreams,

But my dreams became bigger:

That one day I'll become a politician, just like you.

Mr. MP said:

What does that have to do with me?

I said:

I want to be your apprentice!

[He smiled broadly, but I cringed].

Mr. MP said: [To his secretary]

This block wants to be my apprentice.

Can you believe that?

Ha! Me, apprentice a block like her?

[She frowned, but I didn't understand]

When can you start?

I said:

How about tomorrow?

No, pardon me! How about next week?

Mr. MP said:

No! How about today?

[He smiled again. I didn't understand him]

Say, after 4:30?

I protested:

That is after working hours.

No offices are open at that hour!

Mr. MP said:

If you want to become my apprentice,

Meet me at Monte Carlo Club after 4:30 p.m.

Be sure to look good, really good for me.

I protested:

Today is too soon.

Besides, looking good for you is not part of my dream.

I want to someday become the MP of my constituency, just like you.

Then one day, I can become president like Kibaki.

Then one day, I can become president like Ellen J. Sirleaf.

Then one day, I can become Kenya's first female president.

Mr. MP said:

That is not how it works!

If you want to become an MP,

You must first become a politician.

Then after you become an MP,

You might just become a Minister.

But to become president . . .

[He snared]

What a dream! No, you cannot become a president.

Truthfully, being president is not a woman's reality,

Your unfledged brains are not made for presidential duties.

Besides, you have too many issues—periods, children, cooking —

Wouldn't you agree you have more stuff to do than be president?

Your reality, as we know it, is working on your back!

I said:

You filthy dirty rotten scoundrel.

I dreamt big dreams,

But prostituting myself wasn't it!

Mr. MP said:

You devil of a woman!

Get the hell out of my office you crazy bitch!

So he tossed me out of his office to the pavement.

I scratched my knees upon my landing till they bled.

The soil upon which I landed became tainted red.

Sadly, my political aspirations were dead before they began, but that didn't halt my dreams.

[IV]

I gathered my mangled body off the pavement,

Licked the palm of my right hand and wiped my knees.

I boarded a BodaBoda to my sister's home in distress.

She was the beautiful Adisa, the town's call girl.

Perhaps, she, too, dreamt small dreams that became bigger.

Her powder caked face pruned at my appearance!

I said:

> *I have a conundrum of a lifetime.*

Adisa said:

> *Make it quick, Sister.*
>
> *I have no time for your foolishness!*
>
> *You know time is money.*

I said:

> *I know you would understand if I told you.*

Adisa said:

> *Girl, make it quick!*
>
> [She looked at her gold Seiko watch]
>
> *Jonny will be coming soon.*

I said:

> *What happened to sisterhood?*
>
> *Never mind! I had a small dream,*
>
> *But my dream got bigger.*

Adisa snapped:

> *Get to the point before I lose my temper.*

I said:

> *I dreamt of becoming a doctor.*
>
> *I dreamt of becoming a politician.*
>
> *I dreamt of becoming an engineer.*
>
> *I dreamt of . . .*

She said angrily:

> *Shut-up you little buffoon!*
>
> *Don't make my heart bleed for no good reason.*
>
> *Don't you know those were my dreams too?*
>
> *See where they got me, on my back!*
>
> *Now, I have a nice clean house.*
>
> *I powder my face with the most expensive powders.*
>
> *I wear the most expensive dresses, just look at me.*
>
> *I splash my body with the most expensive fragrances.*
>
> *I sleep between white satin sheets—clean and soft.*
>
> *Not to mention, I don't go hungry—fruit of my labour!*

I said:

> *What do you suppose I should do?*
>
> [I interrupted her].

She said:

> *Stop chasing empty dreams; they are not a reality.*
>
> *Dreams are a figment of your imagination.*
>
> *They, too, were a figment of my imagination long ago.*
>
> *If you must chase phantoms, go see Andigo, the seer.*

Perhaps, she can tell you what to do.
They say she can see into the future.
If not, remember what Father said;
He might be right, you know!

I said:

Big sister, Father was very wrong.
If Andigo can help me, why didn't you seek her help?

Adisa said:

That is not for you to know.
No, I'll tell you; you might stop chasing phantoms.
I was too stubborn to listen to reason.
My dreams were my everything.
I dreamt and chased them, but only in mind,
Where they were destined to reside.
Remember this is not about me, but you.
Please hurry-up, or if you are done,
Get away from here now before Jonny arrives!
He has bad manners, and he might want to . . . .
Forget . . . time is money; go away, will you?
And please, don't come back again . . .

Adisa, in favouring Jonny, turned her back on me.
Her dismissal lacerated my heart,
But that didn't halt my dreaming; it inspired me.
I walked away from my sister with a heavy heart,
But my mind still swam with my illusions of hope:
  That my dreams will become my reality.
  That Andigo was my last resort and hope!

[V]

Determined in my quest to realize my dreams,

Which had become bigger and bigger,

I went to see Andigo, the Seer, at her home for counsel.

I hoped her stones of divination could see into my future.

I hoped her stones of divination could be my saving grace.

I hoped her stones of divination could predict my dreams,

Which had become bigger and bigger and bigger than life!

I said:

> *Mother, I have come from far to see you because:*
> *I dreamt big dreams, but my dreams became bigger.*
> *I talked to my father.*
> *I visited my Priest.*
> *I visited my Mr. MP.*
> *They all think I am mad, but I disagree.*
> *I visited my sister- who sent me to you!*
> *You, who is the Mighty diviner;*
> *You, who is the bearer of knowledge;*
> *You, whose spiritual eyes see the secrets of one's heart;*
> *You whose spiritual eyes can unravel the mystery of one's life;*
> *Please make known to me the mysteries of my life!*
> *Tell me Mother:*

Is it wrong for me to dream of big dreams?

[She smiled, but said nothing.

I sat silently and eagerly awaited her response]

Andigo said:

It is not wrong to dream my child,

Dreaming is all women can do in this world.

Dreaming is all we can do in this world.

Dreaming is all that can save us from our lunacy.

I said:

Mother, you don't understand!

Although I am a dreamer, I want my dreams to be my reality.

[To which she smiled as though I was undeniably mad]

Mother, throw-up your stones of wisdom.

Mother, toss-up your stones of divination!

Let them speak to you about me!

Let them tell you of my fate!

Let them speak to you of my future dreams!

Let them tell you about the realities of my dreams!

Can my dreams become my reality?

Andigo said:

These stones are worthless to your dreams my child.

These stones can't make your dreams be your reality.

Only you can make your dreams a reality!

Only you can make your reality a reality!

I protested:

But how?

Don't you foretell the future?

Don't you look into people's hearts?

Please tell me Mother, am I mad in my dreaming?

Andigo said:

Child, you have it all wrong.

I can't tell you the truth about your dreams.

Your dreams are as true as you make them.

You are today's dream.

You are tomorrow's dream.

You are the dream in your dream.

You are the new reality; the new dream.

As for me, I am and was yesterday's dream—

Muted, unmotivated, dead!

But you, you . . .

Puzzled I said:

What?

Andigo said:

Yes . . . really!

Stop chasing phantoms in me.

You are the dream!

You dream of what I couldn't dream.

Know that the dream of womanhood resides in you!

Only you can make it our reality!

Only you can be our saviour?

Follow your dream and you'll find it!

You will see my child, if not today, but soon.

I said:

What?

Andigo said:

I have to caution you though:

That your dreams are not without price.

That your dreams will be your death.

That your death will be your beginning and our beginning.

That your beginning is the end of your old realities,

And the beginning of our new realities,

Where our dreams reside and can be realized!

I scratched my head in confusion.

Andigo's ranting sent me home running!

As I stormed myself out of my mind,

I tore my hair off my head, reclining on my unforgiving cot,

To a nurse's strapping of my hands like Jesus on the cross.

No wiggling on my back could free me from these shackles!

An hour later, the Nurse returned with a glass of milk.

She unstrapped me from my cot.

Nurse said:

Drink this for the nourishment of your body.

I said:

No. It is not milk that I crave.

I crave something greater than milk.

Nurse said:

What is it that you crave child?

I said:

Freedom!

Nurse said:

Hush, don't say that.

It is not possible!

I said:

All women need freedom.

Nurse Said:

That is foolishness from the West.
Mama told me to forget all foolishness from the west.

I said:

I want my freedom and that is all there is to it.
You, too, should crave for freedom.
It will free your mind and soul.

Nurse said:

You are still a crazy bitch!

She pushed me back onto my cot.

She strapped my hands tight and tight and tight,

Till I screamed like a mad woman, but I wasn't mad.

She was the one mad, not seeing she needed freedom,

Just like me, if not even more than me:

For she was a slave to her job.

For she was a slave to Doc.

For she was a slave to her husband.

For she was a slave to everyone, but herself.

I yelled:

Please set me free!
And, just maybe, I might drink your milk.

But she wouldn't budge.

No wiggling and gyrating of my hips

Could loosen my strap tightened hands.

She looked at me with a gleeful smile.

Then, the light in her eyes went out.

Nurse said:

No. Go to hell you rotten wench!

She stuffed my mouth with cotton and stormed out.

I became a mute in the core of the sun:

Never to speak of my dreams.

Never to speak of my Father.

Never to speak of my Priest.

Never to speak of Mr. MP.

Never to speak of my sister.

Never to speak of Andigo.

Never to speak of my freedom.

I closed my eyes to the pain in my limbs.

And in my chained mind's eye,

Mama, my guardian angel, appeared to me.

I said:

Mama, how did I get here,

Strapped on this cold unforgiving cot?

Mama said:

I took you to school.

You loved school.

Don't you remember?

I said:

Aaah, Mama, I see! I loved school.

Mr. Umene taught me English.

Mr. Umene taught me Reading.

Mr. Masita taught me Writing.

Mr. Mlogooli taught me Math.

Aaah, my life's track mapped by education!

Mama said:

That is right!

They were good teachers.

I said:

I started reading books.

These books, in turn, became my undoing,

For which I am strapped on this cot.
Shadrack introduced me to William Shakespeare.
Meshach introduced me to Elizabeth Stanton—
Oh! Yes! 'The Declaration of Sentiments'—
Then, I withdrew into the wandering wonderland
of my mind.

I wonder why the sun is hot.
I wonder why the desert is dry.
I wonder why the sky is blue.
I wonder what I'll wonder next . . .

Mama said:

That is right.

I said:

That is how I started to dream . . .
I dreamt a small dream and my dream became
bigger;
Now, my hands are strapped on a freaking cot,
Chained indefinitely . . .

Mama said:

You can free yourself from your mind's chains.
You are not mad my child.
You are not a sinner my child.
You are not a harlot my child.
You are only a dreamer my child.
Only in your dreams you are deemed these things.
Only in your dreams you threaten the rulers of
the universe.
Only in your dreams you threaten demagogues of
brute force.
Only in your dreams you threaten humanity,
But don't you dare stop! Agitate, agitate, and
agitate!

Thus, in my mind, my feeble mind,
I *know* I'll never stop dreaming.
Even with my cotton stuffed mouth,
I *know* I'll never stop dreaming.
For to do so would be my death!
Thus, I'll keep on dreaming and dreaming:
    of big and bigger dreams—
    of being free someday.
    of women being free.
    of women ruling the world.
    of women relishing their human rights,
    not measured by the wiggling of their hips!
Then maybe, just one day, my dreams will become
my reality.
Then maybe, just one day, my voice will ring loud
and clear,
Beyond my humble Kenyan upbringing, and across
the oceans;
For a Kenyan woman, it is not yet *Uhuru*!

The Dreamer's 'Dream' . . .

[I]

I dreamt big dreams, but my dreams got bigger,
And for my dreaming, I am condemned to a batty
pen,
In a darkness engulfed blue walled room,
Blue like the decorative blue of my wrists and
ankles,
Held hostage under prescriptive scrutiny of a
doctor,
Who, like an alchemist, is destined to unravel my
life's mysteries!

Doctor said:

Nurse, this patient needs a full frontal lobotomy.
I *must find the root cause of her malady!*
[His deep voice boomed.
Giant brown goggles concealed his brooding
eyes.]

I thought:

What?
[The nurse turned to the doctor; unconvinced of
his prognosis.]

Nurse said:

What? In God's name . . . What are you saying?
[Her voice carried with it an element of surprise;
She yelped to Doc's inscrutable prognosis of my
malady.]
She does not need a frontal lobotomy.
*Prayers, perhaps! That might reel her from her
lunacy!*

I thought:

> *What lunacy? I am not mad.*

Doctor said:

> *I am the doctor, aren't I?*
>
> [Nurse shrugged her shoulders.]
>
> *Prepare the patient for surgery, will you?*
>
> [He barked his orders and stormed out.
> The Nurse twisted her nose in disgust.]

I thought:

> *I don't need surgery!*
> *For what? I only dared to dream!*
> *And for my dreaming I am deemed crazy,*
> *Crazy enough for a frontal lobotomy.*
> *I DON'T NEED A LOBOTOMY!*
> *I need FREEDOM!*
>
> [But I understood my squabble to be futile.]
>
> *How could the Doctor understand me?*
> *After all:*
>
>> *My father had not understood me.*
>> *My priest had not understood me.*
>> *My M.P. had not understood me.*
>> *My own sister had not understood me.*
>> *My medicine woman had not understood me,*
>> *Save for my mother, but she couldn't help me.*
>
> *Would a doctor, a man of great intelligence,*
>> *Understand me?*
> *How could he understand me?*
>> *My dreams were my heart's desire!*
>> *My dreams were my cry for voice!*
>> *My dreams were my prayers for freedom!*

My dreams were my all, my essence!

My dreams were my undoing!

His understanding of my desires was an impossibility!

His understanding of my plight was an impossibility!

His understanding of my saneness was another impossibility—

My doctor—my saviour and keeper of my life—

Knew what I needed—a full frontal lobotomy,

But I vehemently disagreed with his prognosis,

For my illness was not a physical ailment; that for sure, I knew!

Deaf as a post, Doc vetoed Nurse's prayer cure for my malady.

Neither could he fathom my saneness, not even if I screamed it,

Nor stormed myself out of my mind: He wouldn't listen to me!

[II]

The clock struck one in the night.

As l lay on my cot, helpless and vulnerable like a lamb,

The darkness, real pitch blackness, of my room,

Like the four oppressive walls, nearly suffocated me,

Eroding the little pride I had left.

I drifted further into the *lala* land of my mind—

Into a dark deep coma-like-slumber.

There, I dreamt, *really*, I dreamt a *real* dream!

It wasn't like in *my* big dreams that had become bigger,

Bigger and bigger and bigger than life itself.

I wasn't in my blue painted room at Mathare Hospital!

I wasn't tied on a cot with my legs and hands pinned into an X;

Instead, I was held hostage in a whitewashed room,

Sprawled atop a cold table, like Jesus on the cross.

The dazzle of sparkling florescent lights shone upon me.

This arresting shower that nearly blinded me emitted no heat!

My body shivered to my teeth's chatter beneath the shower.

An ivy bag suspended to my side was as irksome as my chatter.

Drips of clear white liquid trickled into my veins— my life line—

Drop by drop, by drop, by drop, by drop, by drop!

My listless body, mummified in white calico sheets,
was immobile.

I felt the coolness of the ivy as it snaked through
my veins.

Me, a numb mummified mute in prostration I was!

Above me, hovering underneath this dazzling
celestial like bliss,

Stood a spectre—*my saviour*— adorned in a white
swaddling gown,

Giant brown goggles concealed his biddy eyes,

But exposed his crinkled whiskered face.

Around his neck, a glistening snake-like tube
hung.

Giant brown goggles hid his delight of my imminent
lobotomy.

My Saviour said:

   What is your name little girl?

I turned to see to whom he referred.

There was no one else, but me; so I told him my
name.

I watched him stub a needle in my ivy tube.

He squeezed something into it and watched it drip.

Drop by drop, by drop, by drop, by drop, by drop!

I felt a sting shoot through my vein to my brains.

It was as sharp as the sting of an angry hornet.

What a pain! What a pain! And all for what?

Only because I dared to dream of big dreams that
grew!

A cool tingle snaked through my veins and blood
streams.

As a sinister smile crept on *my Saviour's* face.

Relax pretty young thing, your fate is in my hands.

[This voice of *my God* wasn't assuring.

I felt no comfort from his assuring words;

Instead, a stormy fear ambushed me.]

Do you have any children?

[He probed, gazing into my eyes through his speckled glasses.]

I said:

NO!

[Though I wanted to tell him:

Sir, children weren't part of my dreams that became bigger.

Children and I are like oil and water—very incompatible.

I hate everything about them, with a passion!

Instead, I muted . . . and that was all.]

My Saviour said:

Could you please count one to ten?

[He barked at me, really, like a dog.

Whoof! Whoof! Whoof!Whoof!

I wanted to refuse, but couldn't!

What was I to do if he already had me strapped?

And with the ether running through me,

Through my blood, like a viper's venom,

I was his for the taking.]

I said:

One, two, t-h-r-e-e-e, f---o---u-------

[Against my consent, my tongue went numb,

Numbed by the venomous sting of ether.

Or was it my brain that ceased to be?

I couldn't tell which was which . . .

Immediately, I saw my spirit float out of my body:

> I could see everything,
> But felt no pain—my nirvana.
> I had no speech, for my voice was frozen,
> Like the frigidity of my body to the room's chillness.]

Nurse said:

> *There, you have really done it!*
> *You have really done it Doctor.*
> *You've finally tamed the ungrateful wench.*
> *If only that was permanent . . .*
>
> [She snared. I didn't understand her.]

My Saviour said:

> *I am paid to save lives, not take any!*
>
> [Though, he was really taking my life, literally—
> That, I was certain of! To his heart's delight!]

I thought:

> *Save what life, mine? Not a possibility.*
> *Without my big dreams, am I not dead?*
> *Worse still, even in my dreams, I am strapped!*
> *Tuffia! What a life for a girl who only dared to dream,*
> *Dream of real dreams, of being somebody,*
> *Dreams of being recognized as human.*
> *Was that too much to ask or desire?*

Nurse said:

> *Go to sleep you wretched wench.*
> *Don't forget to say your prayers.*
> *God knows you need His saving Grace.*
> *God knows you need saving, real saving,*
> *Not from anyone, but yourself . . . You hear?*

I thought:

> [Sister, I don't believe in God.
>
> My God is Mlogooli, Father of Logooli people.
>
> I knew she wouldn't understand it.
>
> For that reason, I didn't tell her.
>
> I already knew what she would say in return:
>
> > *Doctor, please give her more ether, will you!*
> >
> > *Don't forget her hysterectomy and clitorectomy.*
> >
> > *O! God knows she is surely out of her mind.*
> >
> > *For her not to believe in Him is sacrilegious.*
> >
> > *Her disbelief is her death . . . Rotten wench!*]

I mumbled:

> *God loves those who humble themselves,*
>
> *Not those who sit on the pedestal of judgment.*
>
> *God loves those who are meek,*
>
> *Not those on the pedestal of crass vulgarity.*
>
> *God loves those who see not the speck in others' eyes,*
>
> *While theirs are lead filled with mountains of logs.*
>
> *God loves those who are persecuted for righteousness,*
>
> *Not those who persecute the righteous and truth seekers,*
>
> *For the unrighteous are doomed to languish in Hades.*
>
> [This mumbled outburst worked.]

Nurse said:

> *Doctor, come quick!*
>
> [He did]
>
> *The mute done shut her vulgarity,*
>
> *Mumbled some mumbo-jumbo crap!*
>
> *Perhaps, you can decipher her speech.*

I thought:

My speech needed no deciphering.

I mumbled:

Let those who are humble and meek
Seek the kingdom of God—
Not those on the pedestal of judgment and
righteousness!
Let this sorry lot hung themselves, for theirs is
Hades kingdom.

[These latter words ran through my brain,
Much like the ether injected in my vein.

No one heard them, but me . . .

Nurse was too busy looking for Doc!

I floated above my body—

As darkness consumed my room,

Like the dark thoughts on my mind.

Real dark thoughts, of harming the Nurse,

Flashed my sable mind and vanished fleetingly;

After all, it wasn't in my nature to do others
harm.]

I thought:

Ill thoughts never accomplish anything.
That is what Mama used to tell me.
Nothing whatsoever . . . Zilch. Nada!
I wondered what she would say to me now—
Would she pat me on my back?
Would she cheer me on?
Or would she admonish me?
But for what, dreaming?

[I watched the surgeon's steady hands chisel my
crania

Like a lumberman at a wood felling—

I felt no pain in his chiselling—none whatsoever—
Permanent scars that talked, imprinted on my skull,
Snaked down my forehead like a river,
Soon to be muted by the curly forest on my head,
Their voice suffocated, just like mine in life.

So, I came out of the chiselling of my frontal lobe,
To soft thuds of pata- pata-pata-pata-pata!
To the gyrating of my hips held hostage on my cot
To the twisting-and- turning of my wrists and ankles
Tied tightly and firmly onto an unforgiving guardrail.
And in came the Nurse, like Inspector Gadget.
Roughly, she flipped the light switched on—
Dull florescent lights exposed the blue orbs of my wrists and ankles
These decorative blue of my flesh showed signs of red,
But no drop fell, leaving my calico sheets blemish free—
To the whimpering of my voice, but no words came out,
Muted in life, just as I was muted with ether in my dream.]

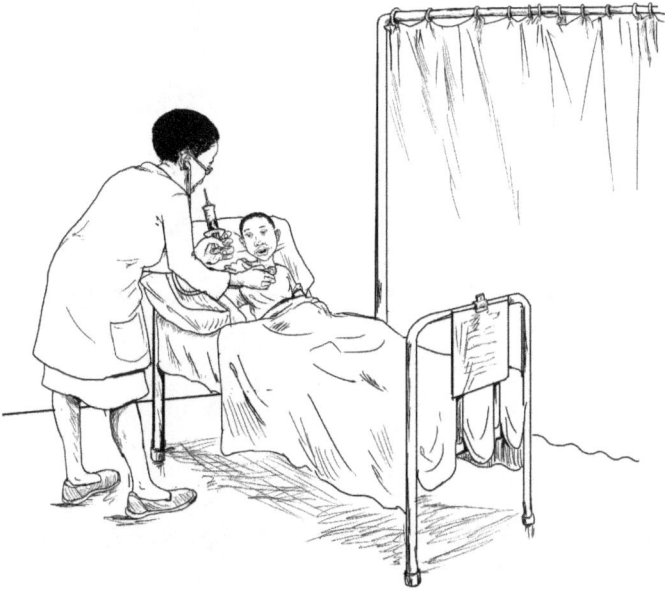

The Dreamer's Reality and Dreams Fused . . .

The sun's bright dawn beams showered my room;
It was the day of my life's greatest transformation.
For the Doctor hurriedly stumbled into my room,
His whiskered face rattled like a caged mongrel.
He neither looked nor spoke to me, afraid I'd see the *truth*;
Yet, in that twinkling, I knew *it* already without his telling!
The whole *truth* and nothing more: My voice null and void;
For I was completely absent as I was present!
Doctor said:

> *Nurse, why isn't the patient prepped for surgery?*
> [He growled as spit spewed from his mouth.]
> *Women! What klutz, hard of hearing and deaf like a nail,*
> *You can't hammer meaning into their small brains; try it!*
> *You will see; how easily they fall prey to manipulation.*

I thought:

> *What a dimwit!*
> *No respect for womenfolk.*
> [The Nurse didn't talk back.
> What a dutiful smart woman!
> Not me! I used my voice,
> Not a smart move, but my undoing.
> If only she could put him in his place!

No, she is way too smart for that.

That would cause her trouble.

She must avoid it like a plague.]

Doctor said:

Get the patient ready, will you?

[He bellowed.   The Nurse warily nodded in agreement.]

I thought:

His tone and attitude irritated me.

His very being irritated me.

Yet, my fate rested in his hands—

Only and only because of a foolish dream—

For which I am condemned into infirmary,

My fate sealed at a doctor's barking.

So, I awaited his unforgiving knife.

Nurse said:

No worries Doctor!

The patient will be ready in a few minutes!

[Doctor dashed out to my shrieking protest.

I wiggled, twisted, and turned my body.

There was no change in my restraints.

The orbs on my wrists and ankles reddened.]

That won't do you any good!

[Nurse warned me.]

Doctor! I need help, in pronto!

[I didn't listen to the fear in her voice.

I continued screaming to my own demise.]

I thought in protest:

I am not deaf and dumb!

If you dared to ask me anything, you would know!

I am not ignorant; don't you ever forget it.

If you gave me a chance, you would know!
I only made four simple requests:

> *To be free.*
> *To be accepted.*
> *To be actualized.*
> *To be appreciated.*

Instead, in return:

> *I am subjected to vulgarity—*
> *Jezebel, a lousy hussy, a dimwit, imbecile—*
> *If words could kill* [and words do kill],
> *I would be six feet under.*
> *It is a miracle I am still alive,*
> *But not for long; if Doc has his way,*
> *I am a goner; a dumb goner!*

Nurse said:

> *I have to shave off your hair.*
> *That will make Doc's job easy.*
> [I knew she didn't want to do it.
> I could see it clearly in her eyes.
> But she had no choice; it was her job.]

I thought:

> *Not my hair please.*
> *Not my hair; for the love of peace.*
> *Do not cut my hair!*
> [As usual, the Nurse didn't hear my protest.
> She only saw my constricted face.
> You would think that stopped her!
> No, it didn't . . . just as she never saw or heard me.
> Me, a mere figment of her imagined self!
> Instead, she left my room and returned with scissors.

So sharp were they, they glistened to my room's
dullness.

I gritted my teeth in disgust again and again and
again,

To the clickety-clack of the scissor's metallic
collusion.

No gritting of my teeth could save my forest, no
sir!

For it was mauled, like a dog mauls meat on a
bone.

She flung her harvest in the dustbin in revulsion;

It was with the mighty force of a satisfied
avenger.]

I thought:

How possibly could I escape this torture?

*How else could I evade Doc's chiselling of my
crania?*

If only prayers were part of my reality,

*Surely, I would drop on all my fours to beseech
penance,*

Penance for my entire life's transgressions.

*But prayers were as removed from me as my
surgery.*

Nurse said:

Doctor!

The patient is ready for your taking—

[She yelled from my room,

But it didn't sound right, not to my ears.

I shrieked and wiggled my body.

Nothing happened . . . Truly, nothing happened.

The indigo orbs on my wrists and ankles
reddened even more.

I gnashed my teeth to Doc's return.]

Doctor said:

I told you this patient needs a lobotomy,

She is too hysterical for my liking.

[Not once did he address me.

For he had already diagnosed my malady.

Not once did he ask me what ailed me,

For he had already predetermined my cure,

The cure for my unspoken malady.]

Stop your foolishness, will you?

[He yelped, but inwardly I wanted to tell him:
    Stop barking at me!

I knew he wouldn't listen . . . So, I didn't say it.]

I thought:

I want to jump out of my mind!

This man surely irritates me.

He surely makes me mad,

But I am the least mad person in this room!

[I resisted being wheeled out of my room.

Really, I pressed my body deep into my cot—

Just as I had done so the bus wouldn't leave my Father!

What a funny incident it was, am bawling-up with laughter:

Father and I were homebound from Siaya, where we lived.

He disembarked the bus to buy me a Queen Cake and Fanta,

For I was so hungry for food, just as much as I hunger for freedom,

The kind of hunger that now gnaws at me again and again.

The driver raved the engine: Vroom! Vroom! Vroom!

The engine rattled and the tires glided on the murram with ease.

So, I screamed and pressed my bottom hard onto my seat,

How foolish it was then as it was now—]

Doctor said:

Get more reinforcement!

[He yelled at the top of his voice].

I said:

You don't need reinforcement, Doc.

For I don't need surgery, please!

Don't do this to me, can't you see!

[I protested, but my voice was still muted].

I thought:

God knows I didn't need surgery, but what God?

Wasn't the Doc my God and saviour?

Wasn't I, in my protest, ungrateful to my God and saviour?

No, I only dreamt of three things:

 Freedom—my life's dream.

 Freedom from these shackles!

 Freedom from this loony pen,

Where I am left to languish in bitterness!

 [No one listened to my request.

 No one granted me my wish.

 Then, my *dream* fused into my reality,

 And my *reality* fused into my dream.

A uniformed set of brute force stormed my
room,
Roughly lifted me off my cot to my resistance,
Which was useless . . . useless to brute force.
Me, muted me, at the crossroad of my life—
Neither here nor there . . . buoyed and
undocked!
They lifted me like a leaf and hauled me out.
I screamed till my voice cracked, only in my
head.
No one heard me, for no words came out of
me.
So, they wheeled me to the operating theatre.
With glee, Doc injected a clear liquid into my
veins].

Doctor said:

I have finally tamed Jezebel!

I thought:

Jezebel wasn't real my name!
To him, I was Jezebel and that was all.
All womenfolk, to him, were Jezebels.

Doctor said:

I must transform Jezebel into Eve,
No, Eve was the reason for man's fall from Grace.
No, my patient is better than Eve—
She, the creation of my own intellect is:
Unblemished, uncontaminated, pure!

[I closed my eyes, tired like an overspent donkey!
Yes, I began to bend a little!
No, it wasn't really a bend, but a tilt.
I fought with every fibre of my body,

Ensuring they didn't see my feeble mind—
Those fools . . . those foolish brutes—
For them to see my feebleness would be my
death.
No, I didn't let them see my wakening spirit,
For that truth would toll their bells of victory.
I didn't let them know they were *about* to break
me:

    Mind, body, and spirit!
Much like a broken stallion.
Really, I didn't want them to sing to Pearly Gates
in elation!
Yet, my grit was no match to Doc's imperiousness,
For soon, his portion, without my consent,
overcame me!
Slowly by slowly, it snaked through my veins.
Slowly by slowly, it suffocated my senses,
Till my reality and dreams fused:

    I didn't feel anything.
    I didn't hear anything.
    I didn't smell anything.
    I couldn't say anything.
    I couldn't think of anything.
    I died and lived to Doc's chiselling.]

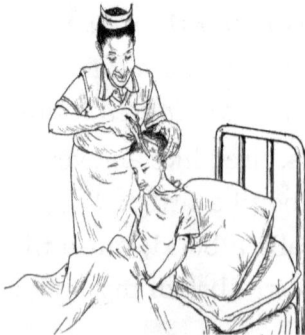

The Dreamer's Unveiling
[I]

At dusk, the rains fell long and hard,
Tap! Tap! Tap! Tap! It pounded my rooftop!—
It unnerved me as it was soothing to my ear.
The heavenly bowels must have truly opened-up,
Such rains of despair, what displeasure!

I thought:

> *What if it rained forever; really, if it never stopped?*
> *Would there be a Noah's Ark to ferry us to safety?*
> *I didn't know why this concerned me . . . useless*
> *views.*

> *After all, I had nowhere to go and nothing to do.*

[The rattling sound of thunder rattled me;
I missed its blinding light for bandages cloaked
my vision.

That wasn't my only limitation; I had limited
mobility,

Lay flat on my cot like a log; no movement
whatsoever!

Not even a twitching of my muscle and Nurse
made sure of it!

Thus, lost in thought, I didn't hear Nurse and
Doc come in.]

Doctor said:

> *By golly Nurse!*
> *We must remove her bandages this evening.*

[He said with the excitement of a new groom.
I didn't hear him call my name,

Though, I was dying to hear it, really!

It had long evaporated from my mind,

Long before I was held prisoner for Doc's scrutiny!

Misted into oblivion that no soul dared to utter!

I even felt like screaming at him:

> *Doctor, just say it, my freaking name, will you?*
> *For the love of peace, just say it; it is not that*
> *hard!*

But I knew he couldn't hear me; thus, I didn't scream—

How could I scream at *my* saviour? That would be so rude!

So, my name, my very essence, remained sealed in his heart.

What a rat's ass, a bumble klutz, to keep my name secret!

He walked out of my room without making mention of it].

[II]

[Nurse watched me all evening long.

She didn't say much to me and I didn't speak to her.

Why bother with those who could not hear me?

Those who were as deaf as the dead and forgotten.

I just lay there in the bubbling peacefulness of my mind.

Suddenly, without thinking, I moved; really, I moved.

Nurse gasped, but I couldn't tell if I scared her.

I had not moved since my frontal lobotomy.

I simply heard the shuffling of her feet].

Nurse said:

That is a good start.

[Her face was within inches of my eyes.

The smoke of her breath clouded my vision.

She ogled into the two open dots on my face.

She couldn't see through my heavy bandaging,

Much as I couldn't see through her clouding breath.

She walked to the light switch and flipped it up!

Dull florescent lights burnt my eyes till they watered.

It was as though my tear ducts were a spring.

The Nurse thought I was crying; I wasn't.

Don't mistake me . . . there is nothing wrong with crying.

I couldn't convince her of it—she wouldn't hear me.

For, I had no tongue with which to persuade her.

It was lead weighted and laced shut as though
glued.
Then, she did the unthinkable; she wiped off my
tears!
For once, she wiped my tears off with her bare
hand.
That was not all; call it God's miracle—her God
that is.
Another unexpected thing happened!
I saw a *teary* glaze in her eyes . . . a *teary* glaze!
Then a light of perceptive depth glowed in her
eyes.]
I thought:

Holy Mother of God! This hag has a heart!
After five years of her mocking my personage,
I thought she wasn't human, devoid of feelings,
Like a eunuch bereft of all manly joys;
Her heart tossed to a dog's ravenous mauling,
Left in its place, an iron-hearted woman,
A cold-hearted hardened wench, but maybe . . .

[Nurse didn't want me to see her tears.
Decorum was important for her sorry lot,
Which she had to defend with all her might.
I smiled, for her iron clad façade was exposed!
I had seen through her *soul's* eye;
I had spotted a tiny tear drop in her eyes,
Even if it wasn't like the spewed river behind my
bandages.]
I thought:

What in God's name was her problem?
Wasn't she free to do as she pleased?
Wasn't she living her dream—a mute Nurse?
Hadn't she hauled insults at me for no apparent
reason?

Hadn't she colluded with Doc against me in my mind's rape?

No, her tears were unfounded—crocodile tears— if I may say.

Not like me, I neither had crocodile tears nor dreams!

My dreams had long died when our paths crossed.

My dreams had long died of Doc's chiselling.

She, complacent in my mind's rape, executed my dreams.

In my execution, I had died and lived to bear witness to her death,

The sting of her death, perhaps, will be my resurrection,

And her resurrection from the entombed abyss of her mind,

My saving grace . . .

I cried:

Holy Virgin!

Be merciful to her sinful soul.

For she, the blessed one, is my peacemaker.

For she, my blessed one, shall be deemed God's child.

[Nurse's head rotated to face me!

Could she have heard my cry? Really, she . . . heard me?

Yes, Nurse heard me, alright, and that is all that mattered.

Don't ask me how I know!

No, I will tell you:

It was the expressed *emotion* I saw on her visage,

> Not like her hard-flat-former expressionless
> visage.
> She, perhaps, a new brood in her dream's
> quest,
> A quest akin to my former, to be free,
> But dead and buried to Doc's chiselling of my
> crania.
> It was the shudder I saw of her body.
> It was the twinkle I saw in her eyes.
> It was the smile I saw on her face.
> It was that profound of understanding—
> Her unspoken understanding of me,
> Still as crazy as I was in my saneness.
> That was how I knew!]

I said:

> *Heaven forbid lest she be deemed crazy,*
> *As crazy as I had been deemed; if not, even more.*
> *Would she find vigour to escape confinement like*
> *me?*
> *For in my mind's eye, I had escaped confinement!*

I thought:

> *What confinement?*
> *Hadn't she been confined all along?*
> *Hadn't she been a prisoner of her mind?*
> *Hadn't she known it then, just as I had!*
> *Unless; she was devoid of reason like a brick.*
> *That would be another issue altogether!*
> *She, my hope and salvation knew her bonds!*
> *She, my hope, knew her mind is her deathtrap,*
> *Just as much as it had been mine from my infancy.*
> *The very atom of my being was as much hers as*
> *it was mine.*
> *So I hope that my hope isn't built on nothingness,*
> *But the bedrock foundation of her reformation.*

[III]

Soon Doc snuck into my room like a thief,
Like death steals stealthily upon humankind.
He scared the dutiful Nurse half to death.
I wondered what would happen if she died.
I wondered if Nurse had lived her life fully,
Leaving nothing behind for Doc's taking.
Not me, I wasn't disturbed by Doc's re-entry.
For there was nothing left in me for his taking,
For he had already taken my all, my life, my being.
I had felt his arrival long before his appearance;
She, who was mightier than man, had granted me
one gift:
The ability and power to detect sound and motion.
Me . . . an adept mute!

Doctor said:

Nurse, it is time!

[The Nurse gasped, but it wasn't a joyful gasp.
I heard Doc dig deep into his pocket,
For my ears were as sharp as a wax moth,
Sharp enough to pick the slightest of sound—
The rattling of keys and coins and whatever else!
But I couldn't let him know I heard his every
sound;
I was as quiet as a corpse in a morgue.]

Nurse said:

What do you need Doc?

Doctor said:

Hand me a pair of scissors.

[I nearly peed in my underwear!

Wait! What if I didn't have underwear?

I heard Nurse fumble with something.]

Nurse said:

Doctor, here you go!

Doctor said:

Oh, thank you dear; this will do!

[He sighed; and then, I felt him lean in towards me,

Brooding over me like a cat over its kittens.

His breathe smelt awful, disgustingly awful.

He touched me; his fingers were as prickly as a lobster's claws.

The two small dots on my face became clouded.

Not before I spotted a glistening snake around his neck.

Gently, he touched my face with his cold rough hands.

And very so carefully, he clipped the bandage off my face.

I heard the snip and a clickety-clack metallic collusion.

In a twinkling, I was ready for a grand unveiling, to his glee.

I pondered why my eyes had been bound for a lobotomy.

I couldn't ask Doc about it; he wasn't the kind to answer.

The lights in my room, though dim, nearly blinded me.

Doc gasped with joy for a task well accomplished].

Beautiful! Just beautiful! Don't you agree?

[Nurse didn't say a word.

I wanted to move my hand to my forehead.

I wanted to feel the softness of my freed face;

I couldn't, but the Nurse did.]

Doctor said:

Go easy on that delicate face!

We don't want any accidents!

Oh! So precious and so divine!

[Gently, she swiped her hand across my face.

Perhaps, she felt warmth underneath my skin,

And the road that ran across my forehead.

My mild temperament saved me from screaming:

Don't touch me, please!

It saved me from being strapped for eternity.

A tamed bitch can't be a threat to humanity,

So, I feigned timidity, with a dead mind and spirit—

And this was to Doc's liking . . .]

Doctor said:

Rest, rest my Angelic Queen, Queen of our land,

May these hands, these divine hands, of thy creator,

Touch your wounded body with the touch of healing!

May the scars of your lacerated body forever heal!

May the scars of your face, like your scarred soul, heal!

[He ranted, as though in prayer.]

Mmm!   Mmm! Just beautiful, marvellously beautiful!

Nurse, be sure to secure the patient on her cot.

[With this elation, he left my room and sanctuary,

Yes, the very altar of my forced prostration.

But not the Nurse; she stood guard of me, as always;

Me, Doc's pearl, his priceless jewel, worth more than life itself.

Nurse executed Doc's request: She secured me on my cot.

An act I thought was completely unnecessary.

I wasn't a flight risk though; after all, I had nowhere to go.

Perhaps Nurse didn't know that, how could she?

I had no home, for I had long killed my father.

I had no mother, for she like my father, was gone.

She, phantom of my past, resided only in my mind's eye.

But with me, Doc's creation and a fine investment,

What was he to do, but have me guarded?

Guarded with every penny from his meagre exploits,

Much like one guards a convicted felon, if not even more.]

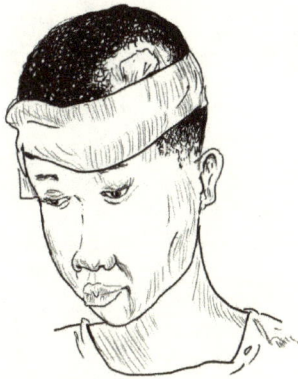

The Dreamer's "Awakening and Death"

[I]

Hours passed, but my dream continued,
Of being free; mind, body, and spirit.
Daylight dissolved into night-time,
And night-time dissolved into daylight.
Nothing changed, my past and present, still dismal.
I was still strapped on my cot indefinitely!
My pulsing present, as removed as my past.
And my past, as removed as my dreams
The very reason for my forced incarceration!
I thought:

>*I had no memory of what Doc had done to me.*
>
>*I had no recollection of it whatsoever!*
>
>*I had no recollection of my whereabouts!*
>
>*I had no recollection of my name!*
>
>*So, had something bad happened to me??*
>
>*Had Doc done something to me which he might regret?*

[I moved my right hand to my face—
You can imagine my surprise!
My hand moved, really, my hand moved,
No longer chained on a guardrail.
I tried the other, and it, too, moved!
I had not *used* my hands in five years.
Perhaps, even longer than that, but I didn't care.
For that truth was unimportant!

Immediately, I felt like jumping out of my mind,

Literally, I wanted to jump out of my mind.

For my hands to have moved, that was newsworthy,

Enough to be published in local papers . . . No!

Enough to make honourable mention internationally!

The title of which would read:

"A Five Year Mummified Mute Awakens."

Alas, hope, real hope, for humanity . . .

Then, I moved both my hands to my face.

I scrutinized them inch by inch by inch!

The azure orbs of my wrists were no longer blue.

They had morphed into ebony, pure black of blackness.

What a disappointment; I had no choice in the matter,

The colour of my wrists, just as I had none in life, my life!]

I yelled:

What happened to me Nurse?

What happened to my blue bracelets?

[There was no response from her station.

So I moved my right hand to my face.

An even a bigger surprise awaited me:

I couldn't feel my forehead, but rough grooves.

Can you believe it? Rough grooves on my brow?

So rough to my touch that it irked me.

I wondered how it got there to begin with.

I slid my hand to the back of my head to my nape,

It was as smooth as a baby's bottom!]

I thought:

Why? Why? Why?

What in God's name happened to me?

Did any of my siblings die?

God forbid, not my siblings; did a relative of mine die?

[No one heard me; I didn't expect anyone to!
For the answer was as moot as the question itself.
I yelled loud and clear; at least, so I thought.]

Mama weee! Mama weee; come quick!

[What a futile try—Mama had long died.
No audible sound, as usual, came out of me,
This was as frustrating as it was annoying.
Without notice, an avalanche of fear returned to me:

> I had no voice!
> I had no voice!

Luckily enough, in came Nurse and Doc.
I wanted to jump out of my skin with joy.
Perhaps, the duo held my life's mystery.]

I said:

Nurse, what happened to me?

[She didn't hear nor answer me.]

Nurse said:

Doctor, you did a fantastic job on her!

Mmmh! Mmmh! Just marvellous! Just marvellous!

No more trouble from her . . . that I am certain.

I said:

Doctor, what happened to me?

[He, too, didn't answer me.
For I was like a visible ghost!

Present, but unheard by all!

Doc smiled and then broke into a rant,

Ascending on the braggadocios pedestal of self-elation,

While I fell through the chasm of self-immolation.]

Doctor said:

Nurse, look at her! Just look at her.

What a fine specimen, as calm as a gliding moon.

She will make such a fine wife, just fine;

Not like the loud-mouthed uncompromising old fool!

She will go out there—multiply and fill the world,

Her God's destined role in society, and nothing more!

I thought:

Did the Nurse approve of Doc's attitude?

[I couldn't tell, but relieved my ovaries were still intact.]

Though I wasn't a fine specimen of man's coinage.

I was as human as they were, that was all.

Though, being a mother had not been part of my dreams.

I drew that line years ago, longer than I could remember!

Any dimwit who knew me would know—

Multiply and replenish earth, Doc's desire of me,

Was his dream, not akin to my dreams that became bigger,

Dreams to which Doc, my creator, was oblivious and remained.

I will not multiply and fill the earth, not in its
corrupt state.

[Doc couldn't see reason—

In his mind's eye, everything he created was
good;

Everything he created *in* me was good, untainted.

In the offing of my mind, he was wrong!]

Nurse Said:

Do you agree with Doc, honey?

[She addressed me, but I couldn't speak].

I thought:

What honey? What an unnatural expression.

[I rotated my head to spot the bee hive.

There was none, not even an open jar].

Nurse said:

Doc, how do you plan to make her multiply?

[Doc didn't answer; though I, too, was dying to
know.]

How do you plan to do that?

I mean, make her multiply and she isn't your
wife?

I thought:

I, too, wanted to hear Doc's response.

Being that I was as frigid as a Frigid Zone deer!

As I said before, children weren't part of my
dream.

Whose idea was it that children made a woman?

Doctor said:

I tell you, I will make her mine!
With my intelligence and her reformation,
We will make fantastic brats, just fantastic—
My prodigies, bright, intelligent, adept, geniuses.

Nurse protested:

What the hell are you talking about?

Doctor said:

Don't fret Nurse, you were not my type!

But she, she is my destiny, and I am hers!

Don't you understand that, my heart's desire?

[Nurse was soundless, but stared morosely at Doc.]

Can't you get this through your thick skull?

She is mine, mine, mine, mine; I made her!

[Nurse's face broke into a delighted smile.

Then, a light of understanding broke on her face.

A confident Nurse screamed!]

Nurse said:

What! You filthy dirty rotten scoundrel.

You filthy poop—ass bag . . . !

[A series obscenities spewed from her lips.

I never thought she had them in her.

A tickle of joy tickled my sides.]

Over my dead body!

Haven't you caused her more harm than good?

And all for what, all for what? Dreams!

All she did was: She dared to dream big dreams,

With time, her dreams got bigger and bigger than life.

And for her dreaming, you testified against her,

Testified at her trial and pleaded her insanity—

In your plea, you killed her spirit and damned her soul.

You knew, just as I knew, she wasn't mentally ill!

And for her dreams, you lobotomized her!

[Now, my ears, which had become wider than a
trumpet,

Wider than an elephants' twitched with a hidden
joy.]

I thought:

What trial? Why was I on trial?

I had no recollection of a trial!

[With my curiosity activated,

I widened my ears even wider,

As wide as an elephant's ear!

No word could escape me now!]

Nurse said:

I remember! I remember it clearly now—the trial!

What a sham, what a mockery of justice—

Her father, may he rot in hell; yes, her father!

How he had forced her to marry that fool, Musa—

That good for nothing son of a donkey!

And for what? Just a handful of cows.

*She was a brave soul, protested the marriage
and all.*

For she had her dream then . . . an education.

Her father said, 'No, girls work best on their back!

*Now go into marriage, multiply, keep my name
alive!'*

*She didn't agree with her father and killed his
spirit.*

*A man took her purity against her will, that was
that;*

She protested, but no one heard her cry;

Did the police come to her rescue? Did they come?

No, they accused her of being loose; she wanted it.

What was she to do against such brute force, such evil?

That killed her quest—her dream of an education.

Soon, evil encroached upon her, grew inside her Because of the evil which had befallen her;

Yet, the evil in her womb was unearthly!

It didn't live long enough to see the delight of daylight.

Her quest for her freedom soon dwindled, for which she died.

No longer pure, she was forced, yet again into marriage—

She, a complacent victim of circumstance, bent to pressure.

A bony toothless man, in old age, took her and felt vindicated,

For he had conquered the invincible, a young poor village girl.

She didn't like it! She didn't like it one bit!

In protest, each time she cooked his food, she spat in it!

Really, she spat in his food, such a small act of revolt!

When she was exposed, he beat her senselessly,

That toothless bulldog that couldn't bite a morsel beat her up,

Until she lost her senses, smell, feelings, touch, and voice.

For which she was judged mad, crazy enough for a batty bin.

And now, you, you filthy dirty rotten rascal, son of a donkey,

You done tampered with her personage too, permanently!

For I have watched you kill her dreams!

For I have watched you kill her spirit!

For I have watched you kill her voice

I will be damned if I let you touch a hair on her again, ever.

Look at her! Just look at her, will you?

[Doc didn't say a word; what a damn mute.

I didn't move a muscle, but was as frigid as ice.

My ears, though, were open in my endured silence.

Truly, I wanted to jump out of my mind,

Support the Nurse in her protection of me,

Even though I was already out of my mind.

The Nurse screamed at Doc, but I couldn't see her face,

I imagined her furrowed brow grimacing with anger.

Then she moved towards me and leaned into my face.

Her clouding breath masked my view.]

Nurse said:

Look at her closely—

A chained and unfeeling mummy.

Doctor said:

And just what do you plan to do about that?

You are nothing! You have nothing!

Though you once were my play doll,
Now, you are just a bitter foolish peon!
Don't forget, I made you; you, my coinage!
No, don't you know you are playing with fire;
If you play with fire, it will irrefutably burn you!
Didn't your mother teach you that?
You will burn in hell; I'll see to it you do!
Nurse said:
Doc, you done crossed the line now!
No, you crossed that line long time ago.
For it is you who has played with fire;
As long as I live, you shall suffer its penalties!
As long as I live, you shall never see peace!
I'll be damned if I let you harm a hair on her again.
And for that, you will forever be sorry:

> *Sorry for what you did to her!*
> *Sorry for what you did to me!*
> *Sorry for what you did to Rose!*
> *Sorry for what you did to Daisy!*
> *Sorry for what you did to Lily!*
> *Sorry for what you did to all women!*

It only took me long to see it,
For I was blind, but now I can see.
For which you are about to receive your dues—
Paid in full—there are no 'I owe you!' Got it?
[Doc rushed out of my room,
A wounded lion he was, to his cub's scratching,
Just a little scratch, not too painful for the
invincible.]

[II]

The Lioness's awakening surprised me,

Its imminent roar's rapture cloaked in mystery,

Remained that barren event in its obscurity to me.

So, I felt vindicated in her thunderous outburst,

Yet, almost anon, intense fears overcome me:

What would become of her; she my salvation?

Would Doc give Nurse a frontal lobotomy, too?

Wrapping her every core amid nothingness and doom?

No, she wouldn't allow it; she solid as a rock, or could she?

What would become of me, a sorrowful river of tears?

Were Doc to make good use of his threat to Nurse,

Would I become that lowest of slaves for man's exploit?

How useless these thoughts were; wasn't I as good as dead?

Nurse said:

> *Don't worry my child.*

> *I have a plan; I have a plan!*

> [She repeated herself as though unsure of it.

> I could tell, for her voice quivered with fear.

> Her eyes, a home of tears, glinted in dim light.

> She, a powerless drifter amid brute force, fell silent.

> Her loud moot voice as useless to her as to my own.]

> *Don't worry my child; it will be alright!*

[So, I gazed into her eyes, her defiant eyes,

Sharp and piercing like those of the big tarsier.

No fear resided in them, only a strong resolve remained.

How could I, fledgling in resolve, kill such a soul?

How could Doc destroy such a spirit?

So pure, so full of life, so full of vigour, so full promise!]

Do you understand?

[I nodded in agreement.]

That is more like it.

[And out, she left! Really, she left me to my devices,

So I fell into my contemplative chasm.]

I thought:

Alone at last, alone at last! What a thrill.

Joy should be my delight, not my sorrow;

Not a sorrowful heart anchored, but unbound.

How could I be joyful amid darkness?

Darkness so deep and so unforgiving,

It lacerated my already wounded heart,

Of not knowing my fate.

Me, a wounded rat, in a rat race world,

Wounded without recourse to man's delight.

Of not knowing the Nurse's fate,

She, a solitary wanderer in an unforgiving world!

I closed my eyes, unwrapped, but bound in my seeing—

See if I could see in my unseeing eyes,

Dig deep into my third eye, where I reside.

And there, in the crevice of my heart,

I imagined my freedom—body and soul unbound.
My wrists and ankles, similarly, untethered.
So, I wondered:

   What would I do with my freedom?
   Where would I go in my freedom?
   Alas! I had no husband.
   I had no children.
   I had no home.
   I had no father.
   I had no mother.
   I had me, myself, and I!
   What a trio!
   Wasn't I better off at Mathare?

So, I pondered: what would I gain with my freedom?

Would I have to lose my life to gain my freedom?
No, perhaps prayers were my only viable option.
And if prayers were my only illusive recourse, then:

   Take me to a world where being free means something.
   Take me to a world where equality of our humanity is guaranteed.
   Take me to a world where my heart can be free.
   Take me to a world where my mind can be at peace.
   Take me to a world where being a woman is an asset, not a liability.
   Take me to a world where mournful souls do not reside.

Take me to a world where my brokenness is not my all.

Take me to a world where the viper's venom is no more.

Take me to a world where Doc's sting is nothing more, but honey.

Take me to a world where I am elevated to glory with the cherubs of glee.

Take me to a world where I can sing my deliverance song.

There, at this utopian haven, I can sing praises to the Almighty:

Halleluiah, I am free at last! Free at last to delight in my life's glee.

So, I pressed my eyelids shut to my heart's ponder,
That hope, that very hope from my abysmal abyss,
At morrow's dawning, shall be my reality, my freedom!

The Lioness's Dream and Protest

The next day, the sun's supernal glory vexed me.

Really, I can't tell you why, but it just vexed me.

Perhaps, it was the absence of true hope;

Or my heart's hopelessness that irked me.

If only that glow's light carried with it my Hope,

A nectar attar of hope, I would've revelled in its splendour.

That afternoon, Nurse returned to my room.

She wasn't as irritated as she was at her exit.

Her large brooding eyes, calm as blast,

Transformed into an unforeseen gloom,

Seeing, but unseeing and looked beyond me.

Nurse said:

My child, are you alright?

Are you in any pain?

[I couldn't answer her!

I remained as silent as a corpse in a morgue!]

I thought:

What a transformation in Nurse's nature?

What had happened to my new reformed angel?

She, my feisty lioness and Queen,

She, the monarch of Maragoli Hills,

Had I lost her in her exit, that sable woman,

She, whose roar had thrilled me?

Nurse said:

Yesterday, I meant every word I told you, my child!

My words, though impalpable to Doc's ears, were potent—
Those very words from the sanctum of my heart—
My verbal promise to you was as good as my written.
[She leaned in close to me, ever so, so close.
I could hear her blood's throb through her veins.
I could smell the fresh mint scent of her breathe,
Mmm! Mmm! So, so sweet and so, so soothing!
Yes, I also could smell the fresh odour of her body;
That same intoxicating odour of my own mother,
Filled me with a sudden crave for her touch.
What a dream for a dreamer's illusionary mother!]

I thought:

What is percolating on Nurse's mind?
I couldn't probe her mind; it could be construed as rude.
Probing her mind might force her to abdicate her quest,
And her helping hand is my only hope, my salvation!

Nurse said:

My child, today you are going to see wonders—
Real wonders akin to David and Goliath!
I meant each and every word I said, syllable by syllable;
A kept word is mightier than a false promise;
Though muttered freely, it carries an unexpected cost!

I thought:

> *What kind of wonders is Nurse talking about!*
>
> *I couldn't recollect what Mama had told me about it—*
>
> *I mean . . . David's story, for I had long rejected everything,*
>
> *Everything religious she ever told me; for its custodians,*
>
> *Those whose tongues sung sweet melodies to the innocent,*
>
> *Those confessed saviours of deprived souls, were phonies,*
>
> *And were the reason the innocents hung at man's cross.*
>
> [Her large brooding eyes were still and distant.
>
> Though she was present, she was as good as absent.
>
> The truth of which became clear to me in a flash.]

Nurse said:

> *This man needs to be stopped!*
>
> *He, an unforgiving Lucifer, has violated his oath,*
>
> *Which doctor dares to breach his professional oath?*
>
> *For his misdeeds, he must pay! No questions necessary!*
>
> *I have contacted authorities! Uuuh! Uuuh! I have!*
>
> *You believe me my child, don't you?*
>
> [I nodded in agreement, even if I doubted her sanity.]

I said:

> *What authorities?*

Nurse said:

> *You will see! They promised to come.*
> [I sighed]

I said:

> *Wasn't Doc the authority?*

Nurse said:

> *That is what he thought! I, too, thought so!*
> *I was wrong . . . I was very wrong!*
> *Doc is not the only authority; there are others;*
> *Those more cogent than Doc could ever be!*

I thought:

> *Mmm! Mmm! Doc, not authority?*
> *How could that be? I couldn't believe my ears!*
> *If there was authority, why had Nurse allowed my torture?*
> *If there was authority, why had she colluded with Doc*
> > *In my torture?*
> *If there was authority, why had she let Doc violate me?*

Nurse said:

> *I am sorry my child . . . truly, truly sorry!*
> *I am sorry for not protecting you!*
> *I am sorry for letting Doc violate you!*
> [In her eyes, a glint of tears formed.
> Then a glimmer of hope arose within me.
> I wanted to tell Nurse: Don't cry for me,
> But my anger choked heart hampered me].
> *I was afraid of Doc . . . I was Doc's slave!*
> *No, I was Doc's whore, just like other women!*
> *For those who were unfortunate enough . . . ,*

Those whose paths crossed his unforgiving conduits,

He killed their resolve and filled their core with pain.

His carnal desire of them sealed their fate.

He cowed them, without their consent, into submission.

My child, don't ask me how I became his whore!

I thought:

Is Nurse a psychic? I was about to ask her that!

How could she have read my mind . . . if I had one left!

Nurse said:

No, I will tell you how;

You deserve to know!

My story, that is . . .

You might learn a thing or two from me:

I once had a dream and my dream became big—

It grew bigger and bigger, bigger than life itself.

I thought:

What? Nurse too? With a dream?

But I dared not ask her . . . she, my mother, now;

It was rude to bother her with such foolishness.

[The light in her eyes returned.

Her big-tarsier-like eyes moved pensively,

From me to the door and then back to me.

I wondered what was lurking outside my door.

She didn't say a word to me about it!]

Nurse said:

I had a dream and my dream nearly became my reality!

I wanted to be a doctor! I wanted to save lives,

Just like my mother—she, a doctor in every form—

For she patched my wounds and my siblings', one child at a time;

She, my indisputable grand saviour, the centrefold of my life!

I told her of my dreams; she listened and didn't object.

She told me: 'Go to St. Elizabeth School of Nursing, Mukumu.

There, there at the school, they'll teach you to save lives!'

'I thought: What a splendid idea; saving lives was my life's mission!'

So, I jumped ecstatically, smiling with glee from ear-to-ear!

For once, in my life, I had a purpose and dream, a real dream.

Mama had no sons so my father didn't object, what luck!

Just splendid! Really splendid! I imagined a uniformed me!

Me, dressed in a neatly pressed sky blue dress uniform.

Upon my head, I wore a pure white hat . . . just marvellous!

Two years in the making, I fell into Doc's gorge,

A surreal world, lured with the splendour of a job.

Me, a poor farmer's daughter and healer of lives,

What bliss, what a delight, of gravitating for the stars.

These stars clouded me; I failed to take off my eyes' blinders,

Clouded with Doc's sweet tongue, as sweet as honey!

Yes! I fell blindly deep into Doc's Grand scheme:

His coveted scheme to produce an impeccable off-spring,

Only that I was not good enough for this grand scheme—

So, he fixed me like a vet neuters a dog.

The fruits of my womb, dead before conception.

Then came Rose, Lily, and Daisy, but they, too, were imperfect!

I had no backbone with which to voice my objection of him.

I simply festered in my self-loathing and diminished self.

I watched Rose, Lily, and Daisy flounder to their destruction.

They were like those lost souls at sea, three biddy lost souls,

Buoyed to the tidal waves of Doc's unforgiving sea of deception,

Till he suffocated their senses and killed their resolve,

Till they lost all their marbles and perished.

Yet, Doc blinded my eyes and hardened my heart,

So, you see, I could neither see with my eyes,

Hear with my ears, nor understand with my heart.

So, I was incapable of saving or healing any of them.

But you, here you are . . . so beautiful, so innocent!

You, my child, my darling child; I'll be damned—

Really damned if I let Doc harm a hair on you!

My inculpability of his capriciousness destroyed
lives.
Now, alone, I am left to make restitution—me,
A lonesome female avenger!
[Nurse spoke with gusto . . . such conviction.]
I thought:
Good grief, Nurse has been thunder struck,
For once she was blind, but now she could see!
She who lays her life for others, truly,
Shall ascend on the freedom stairs of glory!
But was her outburst a mere fluke?
[Nurse's memory bank came to an abrupt end,
To Doc's sudden entrance into my room.
Roughly, he pulled open my door like a policeman.
His eyes blazed with rage, so much anger.
A cool breeze fanned my brow;
Beads of perspiration flew off my brow in protest.
I must have been used to my shackles,
For even without them, I couldn't move.
I remained sprawled on my cot in silence,
As if held hostage with invisible shackles.]
Doc said:
Nurse, you better not be corrupting her.
Just look at her, so calm and innocent.
[Nurse held her tongue—
For a tongue is slippery and more dangerous,
Once it slips, you can't undo its havoc!]
Nurse! Nurse!
[She did not respond].
From today henceforth, you are fired,
Your services are terminated immediately—
Rendered null and void by yours truly, Doc!

I hereby order you to leave this hospital now!

[Nurse did not budge.

A moment of silence settled and remained.

Sound stopped momentarily, and movement,

Similarly, stopped for much more than a moment.]

Do you hear me, you dumb wench!

[Nurse didn't stir, but gawked at him in utter disgust.

Then, she pushed-up her nose and spat with contempt.]

That won't do you any good! You ungrateful wench!

You should have tamed your tongue when you had a chance.

[Still Nurse held her tongue.]

I thought:

Why in God's name won't Nurse talk?

I couldn't understand her, I just couldn't.

If Nurse goes, I, too, will have to go!

Yet, would I be able to walk?

For, I had not used my legs in years!

Yet, wasn't this the least of my concerns?

Nurse said:

I am not leaving without her!

Doc said:

She is not yours for your taking!

Make that mistake . . . and... or else . . . !

Nurse said:

Or else what? There is nothing you can do to me now!

For I've already endured your unwarranted penalty.

81

Doc said:

> *You will be sorry!*

Nurse said:

> *Sorry! Sorry! For what? . . . Not a fat chance!*

> [A tickle of joy appeared on my brow.]

Doc said:

> *Leave now before I call security!*

> [Doc barked, waggling his finger in her face,

> Like an angry threatened dog wags his tail.

> Nurse did not move, her ego reduced to nothingness—

> No ego-nothing to arouse either like or dislike in me.]

> *Guards! Guards! Guards, come! Quick!*

> *Take this scum, this poor excuse of a human away!*

> [Doc screamed, as a buff-looking armed pair arrived.

> Their khaki garb and stern expressions nagged me.

> I recollected how the pair had hauled me out of my room,

> That was the day of my frontal lobotomy, what a shame!]

> *Remove this filthy hag out of my hospital, NOW!*

> *Out of my sight you twerp, a useless bonehead!*

> [The guards roughly grabbed Nurse's hands.]

> *If she ever sets foot on these premises again,*

> *Deal with her squarely! Mark my words, you hear?*

> *She is no longer welcome; do you understand me?*

> [The guards nodded and hauled Nurse out,

Much like one hauls a sack of maize out of a granary.

Nurse kicked her legs in protest and twisted her body,

But her kicks and twists were inept to brute force.

So, she had come in as a lioness, but left as a prickly lamb.

Right away, I felt tears begin to sting the rims of my eyelids,

The humiliation Nurse suffered was more than a rankle,

It threatened to crack open my bones . . .

But, I remained paralyzed by Doc's triumphant smile.

And that day, something significant inside me died.]

Doc said:

You are now safe my dear!

[Doc turned toward me and smiled].

You are safe my Angel . . . as safe as you can be.

Safe from Nurse's corrupting stranglehold.

[Naturally, I didn't agree with him,

But I remained quiet and stock still.]

Rest in peace my dear darling one.

Rest in peace! For tomorrow, you shall be mine.

Uuuh! You will be mine; I'll make your life blissful.

[Doc turned toward the door and walked out in braggadocio,

Feeling as big as Goliath and vindicated in his resolve.

With the pledge of an accomplished conqueror,
He smiled at me broadly; it was a sinister smile.
I hated him with every fibre and bone in my body.
I felt like spitting on him, my true desire, but couldn't.]

I thought:

What a rat's ass!

[Silence came into my room—
And the silence lasted for a very long time.
Then, I cried long and hard for Nurse;
I also cried long and hard for myself!
Then I cried just because it felt good to cry.
Then I cried because my Hope was gone.
For my Hope, built upon Nurse's Might,
Had, in a flash, dwindled to nothingness!
Then, I knew, at Doc's barking, I'd be shackle-bound, again.
Thus, *my* hope, that nectar attar of my delight,
Of my heart's garden, had dimmed unceremoniously.
So, when a spasm of yawning caught me behind my ears,
I closed my eyes in protest, of all my endured pain!
Then, slowly, darkness wrapped its fingers around me,
To the rage, rage against the dying lustre of light,
To the dawning of a tumultuous endless night,
To which I willingly surrendered my heart indefinitely!]

[II]

In my darkened room, my silent heart throbbed,
It was to the soft thumps of my wall clock.
Tick-tock! Tick-tock! Tick-tock! Tick-tock!
What a rhythmic splendour, a never ending nag,
Akin to my heart's never-tiring thump;
And must keep on thumping for it is death if it stands.
Forever thumping like a programmed metronome,
It, like time, never stops for anyone,
Forever turning like the wheels of justice!
So, I lay there, above my cot, in a dark filled room.
In the muteness of my lips, I listened to my clock's dull dings,
Listening and listening ever so silently to the night's tumult:

    To the unsynchronized crickets' noisy chirping.

    To a storm-tossed weeping night.

    To the raging storm's pounding on my rooftop.

    To the dog's persistent barking and racing by my window.

    To the wind's whistling, deafening the clock's synchronized dongs:

    Tick-tock! Tick-tock! Tick-tock! Tick-tock! Tick-tock!

      To my heart's soft thumps—thump, thump, thump!

O what a dread, what a dreadful dark night.
Full of bustle, full of life and riotous activity!
Yet, my sorrowful heart wept for my small dreams—
Dreams that became big and bigger than life itself:

Of wanting to be somebody, not a nobody—

These very dreams had caused me more havoc than good,

To Nurse's dreams, akin to mine, that had cost her her job.

So, what were my dreams all for?

So, what were Nurse's dreams all for?

So, that night, on that tumultuous night,

I made my personal pledge—

If not for me, but for humanity:

That I shall forever follow to my dreams end!

That I shall no more grapple humanity's useless brattle!

That I shall no more grope humanity's peerless rope!

That in that dawning hour, I shall dig deeper and deeper,

Deeper into my callous soul and there, declare my resolute:

I can, I have, and I am!

[III]

That night, following Nurse's unorthodox eviction,
I fell in love with her, she, my lost love of a mother.
For in my dream's eye, dreams that became bigger than life,
She told me her waking page in red with ink to the police,
Of which these scanty recollections of it I hereby chronicle—

Nurse said:

> *Child, I ran to the police station after Doc expelled me.*
>
> *I ran fast as cheetah speed infused my bones in sprint.*
>
> *Only one issue remained on my mind: Your liberty—*
>
> *And for those who might tumble into Doc's pitiless net.*
>
> *Restless I was at my stormy arrival at the station,*
>
> *That I startled the police in my unexpected entrance.*
>
> *The urgency of my mind though had seemed small,*
>
> *Instantly grew little by little by little till I saw the light,*
>
> *In my mind's eye, turn into a full blossomed blizzard—*
>
> *Then, I saw hope uniformed in the decorated badge.*
>
> *So I screamed my brains out to the Policeman's dismay:*
>
> *"My daughter is in danger! Please help Mr. Policeman!"*

The police looked at me with displeasure.

His unnerving gaze gave me pause! What to do, what to do!

Police said:

Woman, what do you want? Aye! What do you want?

You better be not wasting police time; time is precious!

We police have important matters to deal with!

Our time is not fragmented in foolish family affairs;

No foolish female squabble is stomached here!

Nurse Said:

No sir! . . . No foolishness here;

Just a simple request for help:

Please, help my poor girl held captive against her will.

Police said:

What? Who? And where might she be?

Nurse said:

At Mathare Hospital and strapped on a cot!

Police said:

Why is she crazy or something?

Nurse said:

No, only Doc pronounced her craziness during her trial.

You see, she dreamt big dreams, but her dreams got bigger,

For which, she was deemed crazy at Doc's attestation;

But it was a ploy for him to lure her into hospital, now her prison.

Please, save her before Doc has his way with her, will you?

[Police did not believe her.

Doc was a respectable man.

To defame his name was heretical.]

Police said:

Who gave you the right to slander Doc's name?

Don't you know what kind of man he is?

A man of such irrefutable name and fame!

Go away you crazy Mama; you are as mad as your child.

Nurse Said:

Doc is not an angel. Please listen to me; he isn't a saint,

But a dirty rotten crook, a rapist and marauding pig!

[I raved and begged, raved and begged,

Till the man's patience waned to my annoyance,

Till he saw reason in my expressed frustration,

The displeasure of which pre-empted his action.

And, like a wounded animal, he sent me back here.

I threatened my return too if they didn't come.]

Can you believe it! My child, can you believe it!

Me- a sable-minded woman faced the law, head-up!

My unscathed return is proof of society's changing tide.

[In my mind's eye,

I keenly listened to Nurse's tale of triumph,

Even if it was a minute of glory.]

Lucifer Crucified for his Treachery

My dawn opened-up to an unexpected ruckus:
The sun's flaming glare drowned my room;
Behind its glistening glow, soft drips of rain,
Glittery, like diamonds, fell systematically;
Drop by drop, drenching an already drenched earth.

Then, in budged Nurse, like a sergeant at arms,
Combatant she was, save for a baton at her sides!
Can you believe that? Truly, can you believe it?
She pulled my door with all her might,
Drafting in the outside in her entrance—
The outside chillness, the rain, and blinding light;
What an expected surprise and entry!]

I thought:

> *Hadn't Doc barked his orders against her return?*
> *Had the Guards, inadvertently, forgotten his order:*
>
> "If she ever set foot on this premise again,
> Deal with her squarely! Mark my words, do you hear?"
>
> *Yet, here she was . . . in the flesh of her flesh!*
> *Where were the guards, guardians of my sanctuary?*

[Nurse's abrupt entrance nearly gave me a heart attack.

No, the delight of seeing her—in the flesh of her flesh—

Nearly killed me; yet, I wasn't ready for death!

If I died, wasn't *it* a dead cause; really, wasn't it?

What a noble act, her personal sacrifice to save me!

Didn't she know I died long before I knew my name?

So, her presence neither gave me joy nor sorrow!

And as sudden as she had come, in stormed Doc,

Whose mere arrival rattled me to my wits end.

So my stomach muscles tightened like banded steel.

Nurse's face cringed with disappointment.

Doc's eyes moved furtively to Nurse's contorted face.

Then, he rolled them towards me and then back to Nurse.

We mutely gazed at him like one watches a show—

A one man's performance at the theatre of the absurd.]

Doc Said:

What do you want here?

You dimwit, are your ears clogged with dung?

[Nurse didn't answer; instead she looked on,

Engrossed in the enfolding theatrical production.]

Didn't I tell you to never set foot here again?

Didn't I? Didn't you hear my orders?

You crazy bitch, you'll burn in hell!

[I chuckled at Doc's impudence.

Nurse pursed her mouth, but no words came out!]

I am Doc, your saviour, don't you know it?

Me, the Lord of the universe;

You, of all people, should know it!

I thought:

What could she be thinking?

[Doc grunted.   The air in my room became oppressive.]

Doc said:

Women! How foolish they are and hard of hearing!

Don't you know you are playing with fire?

Don't you know if you play with fire, it burns?

[Doc was now trembling with impatience.

Nurse's eyes, of an avenging angel, looked on.

I watched the drama with curious intensity.

Silence fell in the room, but was soon broken,

By a loud roar and rumbling of an engine,

To the screeching of tires as they grounded to a halt.

I craned my neck to see through the window.

A pair of uniformed men stormed the hospital doors.

Those on guard were paralyzed by their entrance.

Nurse turned to me in smile, but frowned at Doc.]

Nurse said:

Doc, who is playing with fire now?

[There was a hint of mockery in her voice.

Outside, the police were already ready for action.]

Police said:

Doc yuko wapi?

[Nurse doesn't answer]

Where is Doc?

[A shocked Doc wondered why they were asking for him.

The guards protested the police's intrusion, afraid to out Doc,

But their brute force was a mere farce to trained arms].

Nauliza, Doc yuko wapi?

[There was power in his coaxing voice,

As he demanded to know Doc's whereabouts].

Guard said:

I don't know! Doc isn't here.

Police said:

Wacha uongo we punda—Stop lying you donkey!

[His coaxing voice, harsh as grating wheel startled me.

Then, two successive blows rang outside, loud and clear!

Twafu . . . twafu and then followed by a bawling].

Guard said:

Don't strike me, please!

Tafadhali—please—don't strike me!

Police said:

Wapi Doc?

Guard said:

Huko ndani—he's inside!

[There was a quiver and shiver in the man's voice!

I watched beads of perspiration form on Doc's face,

For his outing was inventible; I knew it, Nurse
knew it!

Just then, in stormed two armed men dressed
in khaki!]

Police said:

Wewe ni Doc?

[A shivering Doc nodded his agreement to the
question:

Are you Doc?

He was silent for a fraction of a second.

The police's gaze in his eyes was sufficient.]

Doc said:

Afande, shida ni nini—Sir, what is the problem?

[Doc feigned ignorance to the police's inquest,

But they could read his mind like a book!]

Police said:

Nyamaza wewe jambazi!

[Doc cringed to the police's silencing,

Wondering when he had become a crook!]

I thought:

Phew! The rat has finally been cornered!

Guilty as charged! No trial for his sorry lot!

Not even for all his sycophantic coons!

For he didn't give me a hearing in my sentencing,

For he didn't give Rose a hearing in her sentencing.

*For he didn't give Daisy a hearing in her
sentencing,*

For he didn't give Lily a hearing in her sentencing,

*For he didn't give Nurse a hearing in her
sentencing.*

For which, he must face the judge's ubiquitous gavel,

For his crimes against humanity, our humanity:

    Count one six to ten years for fixing Nurse.
    Count two six to ten years for fixing Rose.
    Count three six to ten years for molesting Lily.
    Count four six to ten years for abusing Daisy.
    Count five six to ten years for lobotomizing me.

All, for which, he must serve concurrently, justice at last!

As a bonus, I render my unequivocal verdict: castration!

Put an end to his orgy of disseminating his royal oats,

Such a long overdue just verdict for humanity's sake.

He, the god of entrapment, caged like he had caged me!

Police said:

Asubuhi hii, wewe ni mgeni wetu.

[Doc's jaws fell half open to the Police's words: *"This morning, you are our visitor."*

What a travesty, and a travesty he thought!]

I thought:

I will sing: Halleluiah! Halleluiah! Halleluiah!

Take him please; it will be my pleasure—

For now, he is all yours for the taking!

O! What a jubilant day, what a sad jubilant day!

For today, I sing and celebrate myself—

Even if it is only for a moment, I celebrate myself!

Police said:

> *Na wewe kama mshitakiwa, tunakupeleka jela,*
>
> *Sasa hivi, sasa hivi, wasikia!*
>
> [Doc was silent, unable to affirm his incarceration;
> It was as though he had become a mute like I
> was!
>
> The Police's words: "You, the accused, we are
> taking to you to prison,
>
> Right now, do you understand!"]
>
> *Siku yako ya kuhukumiwa haijulikani!*
>
> [Doc received news of his unfixed captivity in
> silence!
>
> He dropped his eyes to the ground, gritting his
> teeth.
>
> But no gritting of teeth could free him now,
>
> Save for death, which to me was his only viable
> option.
>
> He didn't look at Nurse or me!
>
> He didn't even mumble a word!
>
> He remained motionless in his muteness,
>
> That was before the police poked him to the
> sides,
>
> To whom he looked with utmost contempt.]

Doc said:

> *Mbona . . .* why?

Police said:

> *Wacha maneno mengi wewe punda!*
>
> [The police barked his silence—
>
> *"Stop questioning you donkey."*
>
> Doc's words naturally, fell on deaf ears.]
>
> *Wewe! Twende we mwehu sasa hivi!*

[Doc resisted the policeman's command to leave: *"Let us go right now!"*

Upon which, the man of the law grabbed him by the wrists,

And slapped handcuffs on them, akin to my shackles,

Chains that had held me hostage for years on his order!

I looked on with glee, smiling ear-to-ear, to Doc's frowning.]

I thought:

Finally, I am no longer his for the taking!

What a sad joyful day—Doc incarcerated—

While my freedom, a looming reality, was my life's dream!

Thank goodness to Nurse; she turned out alright in the end.

[Jocularly, I smiled at her, but wouldn't let her know my fears!

Inwardly, I knew she knew, and understood me, more than I knew.

My grateful silence was more momentous than any expressed words!

As I glossed-up in delight, I bore witness to Doc's eventual fall:

A man whose capriciousness was envy of every man!

A man whose mere existence fraught me with fright!

A man whose prowess and might knew no boundaries!

A man whose masked kindness was a chamber of torture!

Thus, Nurse and I were left to bear witness to the brunt of justice:

We bore witness to Doc's diminished manhood.

We bore witness to Doc's unequivocal removal.

We bore witness to Doc's fall, *the* fall of a legend.

So, he fell like a log into the chasm of brute force,

Akin to that which had held me hostage for years.

There he will forever languish, savouring his lost freedoms,

Which now rung much mightier than his imprisonment of me!

So, I prayed for his soul; a single prayer it was—

That he, in his new station, in the dusking of his life,

That he, too, should face a fate analogous to mine:

A FULL FRONTAL LOBOTOMY—whereby his snake—

Coiled around his neck in glitter wouldn't be his saving grace!

So, I watched as police hauled Doc away like a sack of maize.

He screamed, he kicked, and gyrated his hips,

But no screaming, kicking, or gyrating of hips saved him,

Just as it had done me no good before my lobotomy!

Behind him, a smiling Nurse followed with a twinkle in her eyes,

Then, she yelled at me as she embarked on the police car.]

Nurse said:

Don't worry my child; I'll be back for you.

[The door slammed behind her, but this time, I believed her!

Our fates were intertwined and I knew she would come for me!]

I hauled my body out of my covers and craned my neck to see:

Doc's glittery eyes gaped long and hard at my window.

A look of glum was evident behind his glittery eyes.

His lion's strength seemed to have left him.

And I held no filial respect for him, my Lucifer.

Then, calm as blast, I dreamt of my big dreams;

Dreams that had become bigger and bigger,

Bigger than life itself, of wanting to be free!

Then, in my lapsed memory of dreaming, I wondered:

What if Doc's hauling was a dream, just like my other dreams?

There was no telling now if my reality was not my dream,

And my dream not my reality, for both conjoined and disjoined;

Just like Andigo, the Seer, had predicted my end many years ago.

So, I reclined in silence, on my hard cold cot, as hard as stone,

As the glare of the sun's glow light lifted my spirits,
For it was to my mind's buoying truth that:
I had found and lost my freedom in a day's rapture—
Boomeranged to my genesis, dreaming of big and
bigger dreams!